SCHOLASTIC

Writing guide

With interactive resources on CD-ROM

Instruction Texts

for ages

7-9

Leonie Bennett

Credits

Author
Leonie Bennett

Series Consultant
Huw Thomas

Development Editor
Simret Brar

Editor
Pam Kelt

Assistant Editor
Marion Archer

Series Designer
Anna Oliwa

Designer
Paul Stockmans

Cover Illustration
Mark Oliver

Illustrations
Sarah Warburton
and Mike Phillips

CD-ROM Development
CD-ROM developed in
association with Infuze Ltd

Mixed Sources
Product group from well-managed
forests and other controlled sources
www.fsc.org Cert no. TT-COC-002769
© 1996 Forest Stewardship Council

Text © Leonie Bennett
© 2009 Scholastic Ltd

Designed using Adobe InDesign

Published by Scholastic Ltd,
Villiers House,
Clarendon Avenue,
LeamingtonSpa,
Warwickshire
CV32 5PR

www.scholastic.co.uk

Printed by Bell & Bain

1 2 3 4 5 6 7 8 9   9 0 1 2 3 4 5 6 7 8 9
British Library Cataloguing-in-Publication Data
A catalogue record for this book is available from the British Library.

ISBN 978-1407-11256-5

CD-ROM Minimum specifications:

Windows 2000/XP/Vista   Mac OSX 10.4

Processor: 1 GHz	**RAM:** 512 MB	**Graphics card:** 32bit
Audio card: Yes	**CD-ROM drive speed:** 8x	**Hard disk space:** 200MB
Screen resolution: 800x600		

Contents

Introduction: Instruction Texts

The *Writing Guides* series aims to inspire and motivate children as writers by using creative approaches. Each *Writing Guide* contains activities and photocopiable resources designed to develop children's understanding of a particular genre (for example, fairy stories). The activities are in line with the requirements of the National Curriculum and the recommendations in the *Primary Framework for Literacy*. The teacher resource books are accompanied by a CD-ROM containing a range of interactive activities and resources.

What's in the book?

The *Writing Guides* series provides a structured approach to developing children's writing. Each book is divided into four sections.

Section 1: Using good examples

Three text extracts are provided to explore the typical features of the genre.

Section 2: Developing writing

There are ten short, focussed writing tasks in this section. These are designed to develop children's ability to use the key features of the genre in their own writing. The teacher's notes explain the objective of each activity and provide guidance on delivery, including how to use the photocopiable pages and the materials on the CD-ROM.

Section 3: Writing

The three writing projects in this section require the children to produce an extended piece of writing using the key features of the genre.

Section 4: Review

This section consists of a 'Self review', 'Peer review' and 'Teacher review'. These can be used to evaluate how effectively the children have met the writing criteria for the genre.

What's on the CD-ROM?

The accompanying CD-ROM contains a range of motivating activities and resources. The activities can be used for independent work or can be used on an interactive whiteboard to enhance group teaching.
Each CD-ROM contains:

- three text extracts that illustrate the typical features of the genre
- interactive versions of selected photocopiable pages
- four photographs and an audio file to create imaginative contexts for writing
- a selection of writing templates and images which can be used to produce extended pieces of writing.

The interactive activities on the CD-ROM promote active learning and support a range of teaching approaches and learning styles. For example, drag and drop and sequencing activities will support kinaesthic learners.

Talk for writing

Each *Writing Guide* uses the principles of 'Talk for writing' to support children's writing development by providing opportunities for them to rehearse ideas orally in preparation for writing. 'Talk for writing' is promoted using a variety of teaching strategies including discussions, questioning and drama activities (such as, developing imaginative dialogue – see *Fantasy Stories for Ages 9–11*).

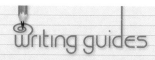

How to use the CD-ROM

Start screen: click on the 'Start' button to go to the main menu.

This section contains brief instructions on how to use the CD-ROM. For more detailed guidance, go to 'How to use the CD-ROM' on the start screen or click on the 'Help' button located in the top right-hand corner of the screen.

Installing the CD-ROM

Follow the instructions on the disk to install the CD-ROM onto your computer. Once the CD-ROM is installed, navigate to the program location and double click on the program icon to open it.

Main menu screen

Main menu

The main menu provides links to all of the writing activities and resources on the CD-ROM. Clicking on a button from the main menu will take you to a sub-menu that lists all of the activities and resources in that section. From here you have the option to 'Launch' the interactive activities, which may contain more than one screen, or print out the activities for pupils to complete by hand.

If you wish to return to a previous menu, click the 'Menu' button in the top right-hand corner of the screen; this acts as a 'back' button.

Screen tools

A range of simple writing tools that can be used in all of the writing activities are contained in the toolbar at the bottom of the screen.

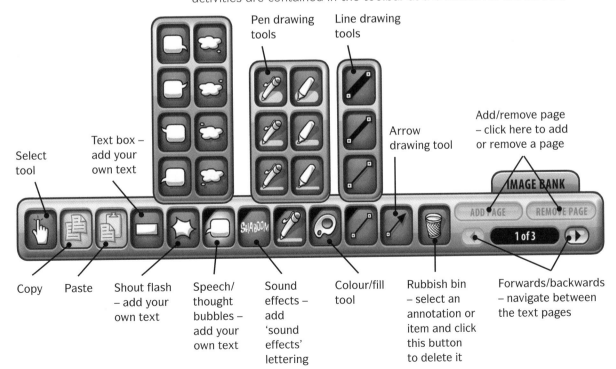

Pen drawing tools

Line drawing tools

Arrow drawing tool

Add/remove page – click here to add or remove a page

Select tool

Text box – add your own text

Copy

Paste

Shout flash – add your own text

Speech/ thought bubbles – add your own text

Sound effects – add 'sound effects' lettering

Colour/fill tool

Rubbish bin – select an annotation or item and click this button to delete it

Forwards/backwards – navigate between the text pages

Print

Save your work to chosen files

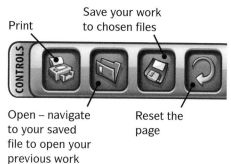

Open – navigate to your saved file to open your previous work

Reset the page

Printing and saving work

All of the resources on the CD-ROM are printable. You can also save and retrieve any annotations made on the writing activities. Click on the 'Controls' tab on the right-hand side of the screen to access the 'Print', 'Open', 'Save' and 'Reset screen' buttons.

View all thumbnails by clicking on the arrows

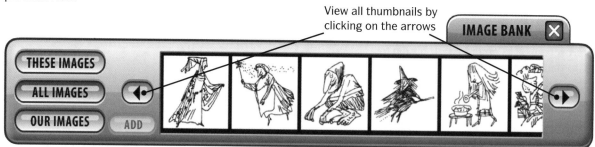

Image bank – click and drag an image to add it to an activity

Image bank

Each CD-ROM has an 'Image bank' containing images appropriate to the genre being taught. Click on the tab at the bottom right of the screen to open the 'Image bank'. On the left-hand side there are three large buttons.

- The 'These images' button will display only the images associated with the specific activity currently open.
- The 'All images' button will display all the photographs and illustrations available on the CD-ROM.
- The 'Our images' button will contain any images you or the children have added to the CD-ROM.

Press the left or right arrows to scroll through the images available. Select an image and drag and drop it into the desired location on the screen. If necessary, resize the image using the arrow icon that appears at the bottom right of the image.

You can upload images to the 'Image bank', including digital photographs or images drawn and scanned into the computer. Click on 'Our images' and then 'Add' to navigate to where the image is stored. A thumbnail picture will be added to the gallery.

Writing your own story

Each CD-ROM contains a selection of blank writing templates. The fiction genre templates will be categorised under the button 'My story' and the non-fiction templates will be categorised under 'My recount' or 'My writing'. The writing templates encourage the children to produce an extended piece of genre writing. They can also add images, speech bubbles and use other tools to enhance their work.

The fiction titles also include a cover template for the children to use. They can customise their cover by adding their own title, blurb and images.

Section 1
Using good examples

Introduction to the genre

Instructions are a very common type of writing which tell you how to do or make something. There are three main elements: a goal (often the title), a list of materials (what you need) and a list of ordered steps (what to do). The main language features are imperatives (command verbs); time connectives (linking words such as first, then, next) and numbers or bullet points to show the order in which things should be done.

Children frequently come across instructions in print (recipes and game instructions) and in speech (telling someone the rules of a game), but they do not find them easy to write, commonly slipping into recount, or writing in continuous prose rather than in a sequence of steps. When aware of the features, children are usually quick to appreciate the importance of listing what is needed and describing what to do in logical order.

Talk with the children about the purpose of instructions and where they have seen or used them. Invite them to bring samples from home. View examples, pointing out the key elements. If they bring diagram-only instructions (such as for Lego or self-assembly kits) ask why they think these don't have words. (*Are they used in different languages?*)

Primary framework link

Instructions is the second in a block of three non-fiction units in Year 3. Within this, children are expected to:

- read and compare examples of instructional texts

- review the common features and make critical judgements about how effective the instructions are

- analyse more complicated instructions and identify organisational devices to make them easier to follow

- research a particular area, for example, playground games, and work in small groups to prepare a set of oral instructions

- try out with other children and evaluate effectiveness

- prepare clear written instructions.

Instructions will help to deliver key strands in the primary framework: Reading – strands 7 and 8; Writing – strands 9, 10 and 11.

About the genre

Structure

Instructions usually have the following features:
- goal – a statement of what is to be achieved
- materials/equipment needed, listed in order
- sequenced steps to achieve the goal
- an appropriate closing statement
- diagrams, photographs or illustrations.

Style

Instructions usually use:
- short simple sentences
- imperative verbs
- chronological order
- numbers, letters or bullet points to signal order of instructions to be followed
- generalised human agents rather than named individuals.

Example 1: How to make a windmill

What's on the CD-ROM

How to make a windmill
- What are the features of instructions? Display only with rollover text.

How to make a sailing boat (part one)
- Instruction text – display only and text entry activity on further screens.
-

Media resource
- Photograph of a paper plane. Use as a stimulus for writing.

In this example, the children will learn the features of instructional text.

- Display CD-ROM text example 'How to make a windmill' on the whiteboard, or hand out copies of photocopiable page 11. Ask the children how they know what type of writing it is. Talk through the text, focusing on the three main elements of instructions: goal or purpose (how to...), what is needed and a sequence of steps.

- Point out two more common features of instructions: clear layout and inclusion of diagrams. Explain that these are typical of instructional writing. Hover over the text on screen 3 to display the rollover text.

- Ask the children if they think the instructions would be easy to follow. See if they can, in pairs, follow the instructions with a piece of paper. Invite them to evaluate the instructions. Are they clear? Can they suggest any improvements?

- Return to 'How to make a windmill' and focus on step 6: and the sentence: 'You many need an adult to help.' Ask: *Why do you think the writer wrote this and what does it tell us about who he/she was writing for?* (children) Hover over the repeated complete set of instructions to display rollover text explaining the key features.

- Collect other examples of instructions and show the children. Ask the children if they have the main features of instructions identified in 'How to make a windmill'. If any of these features are missing, how important do the children think it is?

- Now open the CD-ROM file 'How to make a sailing boat (part one)'. Read it, and then move on to the latter screens ('How to make a sailing boat part one and two' are combined in one CD ROM activity). Ask in what ways these instructions are different from 'How to make a windmill'. *Would they be as easy to follow?* (No, you don't know what you need in advance; it isn't clearly laid out, the sentences are long, and so on.)

- List the items needed to make the boat. Then, count the imperatives to draw attention to what you have to do. Ask the children which words can be deleted to make shorter, more straightforward sentences. What diagrams would be useful and where?

- When they have finished writing, they can print off their work and draw and number appropriate diagrams.

- Alternatively, hand out copies of photocopiable page 14 and 15, 'How to make a sailing boat' parts one and two and complete the activities.

- Go to the media resource and display the photograph of the boy with the paper plane on screen, or print it off.

- Ask the children to explain what the boy has made, then list any materials required. Next, encourage them to write a set of simple instructions about how to make a paper plane. Remind them to come up with a title, use numbered steps, clear language and diagrams if necessary. Then, let them swap their instructions with a partner and see if they can both make planes that fly.

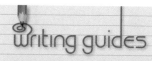

Example 2: Wishford walk

What's on the CD-ROM

Wishford walk
- Examining the language features of instructions. Display only.

A walk
- Drag and drop; writing new directions.

Media resource
- Photograph of school crossing sign as a stimulus for a writing activity.

The 'Wishford walk' instructions allow the children to transfer their knowledge to another type of instructions text – directions. The follow-up activity 'A walk' helps them to write their own directions. Hand out copies of photocopiable page 12 as reference and then display CD-ROM file 'Wishford walk'.

- Ask: *What is the goal? What important information is provided at the beginning and why?* Read through the directions on the photocopiable or on screen and ask the children to follow the route on their copies of the map. Point out structural features (goal, equipment and sequenced steps) and two examples of safety notes (step 7 – 'remembering to close…' and 'Look out for traffic'). Ask: *Why are we told what we pass on the walk?*

- Look at the media resource photograph of the school crossing sign. Ask the class what drivers are required to do. What do the flashing lights mean? *What other road hazards can they think of? How would they mention them in their directions to improve the safety of pedestrians?*

- Next, see if the children can trace the route on screen using the interactive marker pen.

- Talk through the text, focusing on sentence/word level features:
  – imperatives (turn, go, follow) which tell you what to do
  – linking words/time connectives (then, after, now) which help you to understand the correct order in which to do things
  – short, precise sentences.

- Invite the children to annotate their photocopiable page, underlining imperatives, circling time connectives and labelling other features.

- Compare these instructions with 'How to make a windmill'. Ask the children to list the features of instructions that the two pieces have in common and the features that are different.

- Together, devise instructions to get from the playground to the primary school, then ask the children to work in pairs. One partner gives oral instructions how to get from Manor Farm to the post office or from the pub to the playground. The other follows the instructions on the map and evaluates how clear they are.

- Hand out copies of photocopiable page 16 first, then display CD-ROM file 'A walk'. Ask what features on the map tell them the route of this walk (numbers and arrows). Ask where the walk starts and ends (Tim's house). Drag and drop the graphics from the key into place.

- Using the photocopies, ask pairs of children, to follow the route with their fingers, talking through the directions they would give. Then, ask them to complete the directions 2 to 7 on screen or on the photocopiable. Guide them to make precise vocabulary choices and use short and precise sentences, beginning with an imperative. Point out that instructions only include adjectives and adverbs if they are absolutely necessary.

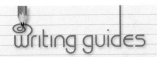

Example 3: How to make a newspaper hat

What's on the CD-ROM

How to make a newspaper hat
- Artwork to sequence; write a set of instructions.

Media resource
- Photograph of simple paper masks as a starting point for a creative exercise.

This extract provides the illustrations for the children to use to write their own set of instructions.

- Display CD-ROM file 'How to make a newspaper hat' explaining that these diagrams accompany instructions to make a newspaper hat. Alternatively, hand out copies of the photocopiable page 13.

- Ask the children to put the eight diagrams in the right order, or cut out the eight diagrams on the sheet, working in pairs. Provide a piece of newspaper which they can use to check their work. As a shared activity, agree the correct sequence. (D, A, E, H, C, B, F, G.)

- Ask pairs of children to each focus on one diagram and orally rehearse instructions to accompany it. Suggest vocabulary to help them: paper, fold, unfold, middle point, triangle, crease, corner, edge, decorate.

- On the whiteboard, display the diagrams in the correct order. As a shared activity, compose instructions to go with each diagram or ask children to write them the photocopiable underneath each diagram.

- Invite the children to look at the photograph of the paper masks and come up with their own instructions on what to do, and then evaluate them, using what they have learned.

Poster: 'Tips for writing instructions'

What's on the CD-ROM

Tips for writing instructions
- Read and discuss the information on the poster. Roll over the text to reveal more information.

The poster on page 18 and on the CD-ROM offers advice for how to write instructions and contains various instructions. After studying the poster, the children can use their new understanding of the significant features to complete the activity on photocopiable page 17 'What's special about instructions?'

- Display CD-ROM file 'Tips for writing instructions' Roll over each question and work through the tips as they appear on-screen. Ask the children to suggest examples of other goals.

- Propose a simple set of instructions (for example, how to wash your hands) and ask them to talk about each point in pairs. Discuss their ideas as a class and write a set of instructions. Select someone to try them out to see if they work. Individually ask the children to identify the goals and the imperatives. Alternatively, hand out copies of photocopiable page 18 and work through the tips on paper.

- Encourage the children to find examples of instructions around the classroom or school. Ask: *In what ways do your examples follow the tips on the poster? How could you improve them?*

- When familiar with the poster, display and explain the activity 'What's special about instructions?' (photocopiable page 17). Talk through the list of features in the left-hand column, discussing whether they figure in each of the three examples. Help the children to see that 'How to make a windmill' tells you what to do but not why. In pairs ask them to fill in the rows with 'yes' or 'no' as appropriate.

Example 1: How to make a windmill

You will need

- a piece of stiff paper, 20cm square
- a pin or a long drawing pin
- a length of thin wood or bamboo
- a small bead
- glue
- scissors
- a pencil.

What to do

1. First, fold the paper in half. Then fold it in half again the other way to find the middle.

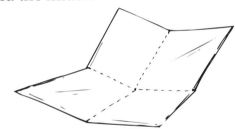

2. Draw four curved lines as shown in the diagram below. Cut along each line.

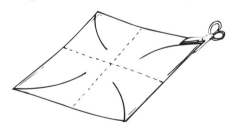

3. Next, fold in each of the corners. Glue them over the middle.

4. Let the glue dry. Then make a hole in the middle of the windmill.

5. Now carefully push the pin through the hole. Then place the bead on the end of the pin.

6. Push the pin into the wood. You may need an adult to help. Make sure the windmill can move freely.

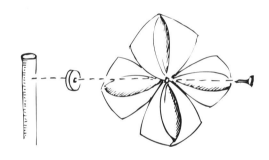

7. Finally, blow on the side of your windmill or hold it in the wind. Watch it go round.

Illustrations © 2001, Sarah Warburton.

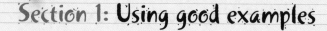
Section 1: Using good examples

Example 2: Wishford walk

You will need: Wellington boots if it has been raining

Start – Wishford Primary School   **Length of walk** – 2km

Time – approximately one hour

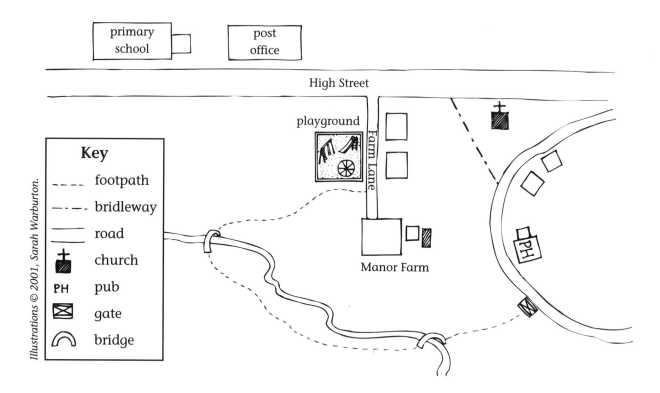

Illustrations © 2001, Sarah Warburton.

1 Turn left down High Street.

2 Go past the post office. Then, turn right down Farm Lane.

3 After the playground, turn right down a footpath.

4 Now follow the footpath to the bridge.

5 Cross the bridge and turn left. Follow the footpath to the next bridge.

6 Cross the bridge and continue to a gate.

7 Go through the gate (remembering to close it behind you) and turn left onto a minor road. Look out for traffic.

8 Go past the Lamb pub. After that, turn left down a bridleway. Follow the bridleway back to Wishford High Street. Pass the church on your right.

9 At High Street, turn left. Follow the road back to the school.

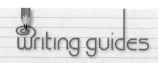

Extract 3: How to make a newspaper hat

Illustrations © 2009, Mike Phillips.

How to make a sailing boat (part one)

● Rewrite these instructions so they are easy to follow. Use the headings 'What you need' and 'What to do'. Write in short, clear sentences and put each new instruction on a new line.

You will need to cut a small piece of paper about 7cm by 6cm. This will be your sail and you can colour it if you want to. Then you should get a toothpick and use it to make a hole at the top and at the bottom of the sail. The next thing to do is to put the toothpick through the holes. Bunch the sail up a bit to make it puff out like a real sail. Next find an empty matchbox. You will only need the tray inside so you can throw away the cover. The last thing to do is to fix your sail to the tray of the matchbox using Blu-Tack or modelling clay. Now you can float your boat on some water. You might like to blow on the sail to make the boat move.

How to make a sailing boat (part two)

What you need

_____

_____

_____

4. Bunch

_____

_____

_____

What to do

1. Cut _____

_____

_____

5. Fix

_____

_____

_____

2. Make a hole _____

_____

_____

6. Float

_____

_____

_____

3. Put _____

_____

_____

7. Blow

_____

_____

_____

A walk

- Start at Tim's house and write the instructions for this walk.
- Think of a title that shows the aim of the instructions.

Title: _____

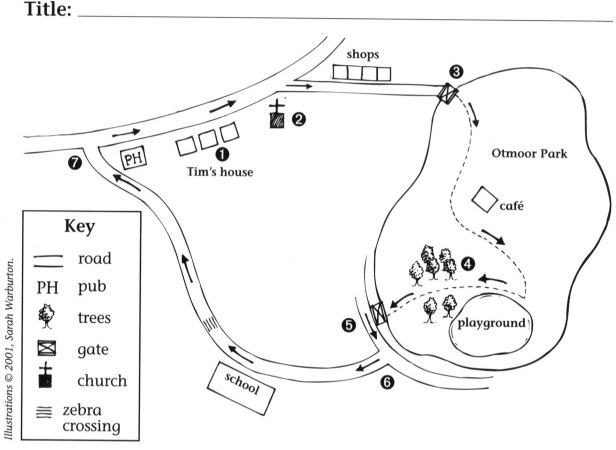

Illustrations © 2001, Sarah Warburton.

Key

——	road
PH	pub
🌳	trees
⊠	gate
✝	church
≣	zebra crossing

1. Come out of Tim's house and turn right.

2. _____

3. _____

4. _____

5. _____

6. _____

7. _____

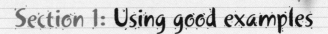
What's special about instructions?

- Can you find these features in each piece of writing?
- Put a tick if you can or a cross if you can't.

Checklist	How to make a windmill	Wishford walk	How to make a newspaper hat
simple sentences			
numbered points			
lots of adjectives			
tells you what to do			
tells you why to do it			
past tense			
imperatives			
time connectives (such as 'then' and 'next')			
clear layout			
tries to persuade you to do something			

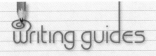

Section 1: Using good examples

Tips for writing instructions

What is the purpose of your instructions?

State your goal clearly. This is often the title:

'How to brush your teeth' or 'Making a kite'.

Who are your instructions for?

Is it for a child?

If so, do you need to include warnings about sharp objects or traffic or working with an adult?

Before you write, think carefully.

What will be needed?

In what order should things be done?

Will diagrams help to make your instructions clear?

When you are writing:

Begin each step with a time connective (first, then, after that…) or an imperative (cut, mix, fold…).

Use simple words.

Make sure your sentences are clear and precise.

Use numbers, letters or bullet points, to show the order in which things should be done.

When you have written a first draft:

Ask someone to try out your instructions to check if they are clear and if they work.

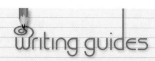
writing guides

Section 2
Developing writing

Introduction: Developing instruction writing

The children should now be familiar with the typical structure of instructional text: a statement of the goal, a list of materials needed, a series of sequenced steps telling you what to do, a diagram or illustration.

The activities in this section will prepare the children for writing their own instructions. They will explore the various occasions when people use instructions and go on to research examples of the range of instructions. The children then move on to tasks specifically related to the features of instruction writing. These involve ordering steps in sequence, listing equipment needed, rewriting a discursive description as a set of concise instructions, interpreting a sequence of diagrams and writing instructions to accompany them. By working on scaffolded activities and using writing frames, confidence in handling these aspects of the genre will increase. Children will develop awareness of the following writers' knowledge (Developing Early Writing (DfEE 2001) pages 152–155):

- Before writing instructions be clear about what is needed and what has to be done, in what order.

- Think about the reader, their age and ability needs to be considered. You may have to avoid technical language or use simple diagrams.

- The title should explain what the instructions are about.

- Explain when they are needed and for whom they are best suited.

- Use bullet points, numbers or letters to help the reader.

- Use short clear sentences.

- Use an end statement to wrap up the writing, evaluating their usefulness.

- Make writing friendly by using 'you', or more formal by giving orders.

- Use adjectives and adverbs only when needed.

- Tantalise the reader, for example 'The best game in the world… '.

- Ask yourself: Could someone who knows nothing about this use these instructions? Would diagrams or illustrations make them clearer?

If the children bring in examples, make a wall display which highlights the common features of instruction texts.

Instructions features

Structure

Language features

Activity 1: Who needs instructions?

Objective

To use knowledge of different organisational features of texts to find information effectively (Year 4, Strand 7).

What's on the CD-ROM

Media resource
- Audio clip: a description of how to make fairy cakes.

What to do

- Display an enlarged photocopy of photocopiable page 25 'Who needs instructions?' Explain that the texts are extracts from four different sets of instructions. Some are written texts; others are spoken words.

- Read through each extract and ask the children to speculate where they have come from. Where would they read or hear these instructions? (For example, A = recipe book) What is the purpose of each text? (The text in boxes will give them clues.)

- Hand out copies of the same photocopiable. Ask the children to complete the sentences at the bottom of the page to state the aim of each. For example, B tells you how to brush your teeth.

- Encourage the children to research the range of instructions in their environment, both at school and home, then discuss their findings.

- Play the audio clip and explain that this is a description in the first person in the past tense of a simple recipe. Listen to the clip and ask for any ways in which it could be improved or changed. If you have time, make the cakes in a cookery class!

Activity 2: This is what you do

Objective

To identify how different texts are organised (Year 3, Strand 7).

What to do

- Hand out photocopies of photocopiable page 26 'This is what you do'. Tell the children that this text is a set of instructions that has got muddled up. Read it through and invite them to suggest what they think it is about. Ask: *Which word tells you which instruction should be number 1?* (First.)

- Ask the children to cut out the individual instructions. Tell them to discuss which instruction is likely to come second, third and so on and to arrange them in order.

- When they have decided on an order, one partner should read out the instructions and the other should listen carefully to evaluate whether the set of steps now makes sense.

- Tell the children that you want them to write a title (state the aim) and a 'what you need' list for the conker game. They can do this on an A3 sheet of paper onto which they have previously glued their instructions, in order.

- Remind them to read through the instructions carefully to pick out all the items needed, including a sharp instrument.

- The next stage is to discuss with a partner what diagrams would be useful. These should be drawn and numbered to correspond with the appropriate instruction.

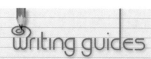

Activity 3: Soup for a mean monster

Objective

To choose and combine words and other features for particular effects (Year 4, Strand 9).

What's on the CD-ROM

Soup for a mean monster
- Text entry activity based on a recipe.

What to do

- Explain to the children that, although instructions are non-fiction, you may find some in a fictional setting. Provide some interesting examples, such as 'Magic spells', 'How to fly an alien spaceship', and ask them to suggest others.

- Display CD-ROM file 'Soup for a mean monster' or hand out copies of photocopiable page 27. Point out the headings 'Ingredients' and 'Method' and ask what sort of instructions these are. (Recipe.)

- Ask the children to complete the 'Ingredients' list. Encourage them to make the recipe as weird or funny as they can.

- Remind them about time connectives (for example, now, first, then), imperatives (verbs that tell you to do something) and the need to write in short sentences with essential information and straightforward language. and the instructions.

- Then, set the children at a computer, and complete the text entry activity, or complete the photocopiable sheet.

- Ask several children to share their finished versions, and discuss their use of the correct language features.

Activity 4: Which way is best?

Objective

To identify success criteria and use them to evaluate writing (Year 3, Strand 9).

What's on the CD-ROM

Media resource
- Photograph of a simple robot costume as a stimulus for class work.

What to do

- Ask the children to recap the important features of instructional writing. (Clear layout, imperatives, short sentences, easy to follow.)

- Display an enlarged version of photocopiable page 28 'Which way is best?' Explain that the chart has three versions for each instruction.

- Working in pairs with a copy of photocopiable page 28, the children should read and discuss all of the options. It will not always be easy to decide which is best, but they should be able to justify their choices.

- Discuss the children's views in a plenary session, asking pairs to explain why they chose the versions they did.

- Display the photograph of the robot costume made out of recycled materials. Ask: *What is it? What is it made out of?* Then ask the children to invent their own list of instructions of how to make the robot costume, including a list of what you need, and what to do.

- See if they can come up with some interesting variations, such as adding antennae, or robotic arms made out of coat-hangers.

- In groups, set the class the task of making robots, then returning to their instructions to see if they can improve their work. Remind the children to use clear sentences, imperatives and short sentences.

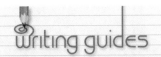

Activity 5: Paper presents

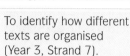

Objective

To identify how different texts are organised (Year 3, Strand 7).

What's on the CD-ROM

Paper presents
- A variety of activities including text entry and sequencing, based on a craft project.

What to do

- Display CD-ROM file 'Paper presents' on the whiteboard. Study the diagrams and complete a list of what is needed for the craft project. The children can use photocopiable page 29 as a reference.

- Next, work through the jumbled up steps of instructions and ask the children to put them in the right order. Can they guess what is going to be made yet? (paper beads)

- Remind them that not everything that is needed is mentioned in the instructions (for example, scissors to cut the paper).

- On the photocopiable, look at 'what to do', then ask the children to find two short sentences. Then ask: *Which are the imperative verbs? Which words tell you when to do things?*

- Challenge the children to think of an encouraging end statement to wrap up the writing – such as, 'Enjoy wearing it!' or 'Fun presents for your friends!'

- In a plenary, ask the class what else you could use instead of a knitting needle (a pencil, a toothpick and so on). They could also add some ideas of their own about different projects involving beads.

- Hand out copies of photocopiable page 29 and complete the activities on paper.

Activity 6: Chunky chips

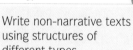

Objective

Write non-narrative texts using structures of different types (Year 3, Strand 9).

What to do

- Hand out photocopies of photocopiable page 30 'Chunky chips'. Read through the explanation of how to make chunky chips.

- Invite the children to suggest, why it doesn't work as a set of instructions. Help them to see that parts of the text should be cut out because they are not important. Also point out that the sentences don't all fit the genre as they are not written in the right way. For example, 'Last time I did this…' is in the past tense and is too personal. 'Lots of people…' and 'My mum…' are too chatty. There are very few imperatives and it is hard to find out what you need.

- Ask them to go through the text, marking it up – putting a line through text they don't need and numbering the separate instructions.

- On a fresh sheet of A4, ask them to start writing out an improved set of instructions. Refer back to the poster, 'Tips for writing instructions' (photocopiable page 18) for guidance.

- Ask the children if they think diagrams would be helpful and why. They can stick their written instructions or a printout onto A3 paper and add numbered diagrams.

Activity 7: How to make a simple tent

Objective

Write non-narrative texts using structures of different types (Year 3, Strand 9).

What's on the CD-ROM

How to make a simple tent
- Labelling and sequencing activity using on-screen diagrams.

What to do

- Talk about the fact that instructions are sometimes expressed in the form of diagrams only. The children may have seen such instructions accompanying Lego models or self-assembly furniture at home. If possible, look at some examples together.

- Display CD-ROM file 'How to make a simple tent'. Ask the children to talk through these diagrams with a partner. Ask them to label the items using the drag arrows.

- Next, look at the diagrams. Establish that they are not in the right order. Ask the children, still in pairs, to sequence the drawings correctly.

- Finally, when they are sure they know what the various steps are, they should prepare a full set of written instructions. They may want to add a note saying to whom this 'tent' is best suited, for example, 'Young children will enjoy playing in this tent'.

- Alternatively, hand out copies of photocopiable page 31 and complete the activity.

- As a class, discuss the end result. Ask: *Was it easy to describe what to do? Do the instructions work without words? Are they as effective with words only – without any diagrams?*

Activity 8: Wiggling worms

Objective

To interrogate texts to deepen and clarify understanding and response (Year 4, Strand 8).

What to do

- Point out to the children that following some instructions will involve time, space or expensive materials or may be very messy. Can they think of examples? (Growing potatoes requires space, making paper is messy, making silver jewellery is expensive.) Instructions should include information to help the reader decide to go ahead.

- Hand out copies of photocopiable page 32 'Wiggling worms'. Read step 1 and talk about what a wormery might be. Then read the rest of the instructions. Were they correct in their prediction as to the purpose of a wormery? Challenge them to think about the practicalities involved in following these instructions.

- Set the children in pairs and ask them to discuss and write answers to the four questions. They should realise that making a wormery is a messy job and that you need to observe the wormery over several weeks to find out about how worms live. This might lead them to include an instruction to spread newspaper on the floor if they are making it indoors, to ask adults if they mind having worms in the house, to point out the length of time needed and so on.

- Ask the children to suggest an inviting introductory sentence, such as, *Have you ever wondered what worms do underground?*

Activity 9: Now it's your turn...

Objective

To use layout, format graphics and illustrations for different purposes (Year 3, Strand 9).

What's on the CD-ROM

Now it's your turn ...
- Text entry and drag arrow activities based on how to make a wormery.

What to do

- Recap photocopiable page 32 'Wiggling worms' and make sure the children each have a copy to refer to.

- Set the children on individual computers and display CD-ROM file 'Now it's your turn...'. Ask them to re-read the instructions and complete the list of 'what you need'.

- Then ask the children to look closely at the three illustrations and match them to the correct instruction, then print out their sheet.

- Alternatively, give out copies of photocopiable page 33 and ask them to complete it.

- Remind them that diagrams should be very simple and clear, and look at different examples.

- Finally, ask the children to draw their own diagrams on a separate sheet of paper to accompany instructions 3 and 4 ('Water well.' and 'Put in about 12 worms.'). They should show that they understand what happens in the process of making a wormery and understand how to illustrate their instructions to assist the reader.

Activity 10: How to make mini pizzas

Objective

To use layout, format graphics and illustrations for different purposes (Year 3, Strand 9).

What's on the CD-ROM

How to make mini pizzas
- Text entry and roll over activities using a simple recipe, focusing on effective use of diagrams.

What to do

- Recipes are a common type of instruction text and offer a clear example of the features of the genre. Talk about the fact that some instructions would be very difficult to follow without the accompanying diagrams. Look back, for example, at Example 3 'How to make a newspaper hat' on page 13.

- Display the CD-ROM file 'How to make mini pizzas', then hand out photocopies of page 34 as reference.

- Read through the full list of ingredients on the photocopiable, and ask children to complete the list on screen.

- Using the photocopiable, and ask the children to match each diagram to the appropriate instruction.

- Next, read the instructions together on screen. As you roll over the text, definitions of the key features appear, starting with the title. Discuss each one as a class as follows: step-by-step details, time connectives, imperative verbs, numbered points and helpful diagrams, explaining as you go.

- On the board, draw up a list of the key points in the form of a checklist. Later, in shared, guided or independent writing, use this to support the composition and layout of instructions to help the children to evaluate their work.

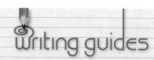

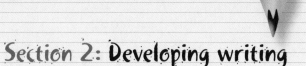

Who needs instructions?

● Where are these extracts taken from? What are their aims?

A

4. Click on the arrow pointing down.
5. Click on a spaceship.
6. Drag the spaceship to the planet. Place it where you want.

B

Squeeze toothpaste onto your brush. Run cold water over it and turn off the tap. Then brush your teeth up and down for two minutes.

C

1. Fold the paper in half.
2. Open it out. Then fold in the two top corners.

D

1. Go outside quickly.
2. Walk. Do not run.
3. Wait outside. Do not go back inside until you are told it is safe.

Clues

> *fire drill*

> *paper plane*

> *brush your teeth*

> *outer-space computer game*

A tells you _____

B tells you _____

C tells you _____

D tells you _____

Illustrations © 2001, Sarah Warburton.

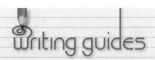

This is what you do

- Cut out these instructions and put them in the correct order.

Wrap the string of your conker around one hand.

Then, put a string through the hole. Tie a knot in one end.

First, make a small hole through the middle of a conker.

Jerk your conker down to hit the other player's conker. The aim is to break it.

Swap places. The other player tries to hit your conker.

Pull back the conker in the other hand.

The other player holds up his or her conker by its string.

writing guides

Soup for a mean monster

- Complete the list of ingredients below. Use your imagination and have some fun.
- In steps 1 and 5 of the method, write a time connective.
- Rewrite step 2 as two short sentences.
- In steps 3 and 4, write an imperative verb.
- Write your own instructions for steps 6 and 7.

Ingredients

_____ very slimy slugs

_____ smelly socks

one large _____

three _____

two _____

Method

1. _____ , put a big pot on the fire.

2. Now you must fill the pot up with water and drop in the smelly socks and stir them round and round with a spoon for ten minutes.

_____

_____

3. _____ the very slimy slugs.

4. _____ them into the pot.

5. _____ , add the other ingredients.

6. _____

7. _____

Which way is best?

• There are three versions of each instruction. Which is clearest? Write out a full set of instructions using the best versions.

How to wash a car

What you need: bucket, sponge, warm water, car soap or washing up liquid, hose connected to cold water tap.

What to do:

1	First turn on the tap and fill your bucket about three-quarters full.	It is best to use warm water but don't fill the bucket too full or you won't be able to carry it to the car.	First fill your bucket three-quarters full with warm water.
2	Put a small amount of soap into the water.	Carefully, put a small amount of soap into the warm water and swirl it around gently.	Now put some soap into the water being careful not to use too much.
3	We always wash the car from top to bottom.	Wash the car, working from top to bottom.	Now it is time to wash the car. I suggest you work from top to bottom.
4	Scrubbing hard will scratch the car.	You should never scrub at ingrained dirt because you will scratch the paintwork off the car.	Never scrub the car as you will scratch it.
5	Get the soap off.	Spray cold water all over the car to rinse it thoroughly.	Use the hose to rinse the car.
6	Finally dry the car with an old towel.	Drying the car will get rid of any unsightly streaks.	I usually find that it is best to dry the car thoroughly with an old towel.

Paper presents

● Look at the diagrams below. Write a title, then list the materials you need. Number the diagrams in the correct order:

Title: _____

What you need:

_____

_____

_____

_____

● Read the instructions and answer the questions:

What to do

1. First, cut strips of paper about 30cm by 2cm.

2. Next, spread glue on one side of a paper strip.

3. Roll the strip of paper around the knitting needle. Keep the glued side on the inside.

4. Slip the bead off the needle.

5. Paint the beads.

6. Then, thread string through the beads to make jewellery.

● Underline two short sentences.

● List the imperative verbs below.

_____

● Which words tell you when to do things?

_____

Illustrations © 2001, Sarah Warburton.

Chunky chips

- Rewrite this text as a set of instructions.

This is how to make chunky chips. First you must heat the oven to 200°C. Then you get 450g of potatoes and wash them. After you have washed the potatoes, use a sharp knife to cut them in half. Be careful! Next you cut the potatoes again. This time, cut them into wedges.

Find a metal baking tray and some oil. Use a pastry brush with oil on it to brush oil onto the baking tray. Last time I did this I spilt the oil and Mum went mad. When I had oiled the baking tray I laid out the potato wedges. The next thing to do is to brush some oil onto the potatoes. Lots of people like to put some salt and pepper on the potatoes before they go into the oven.

My mum usually puts the potatoes on the top shelf of the oven. She leaves them in for about 20 minutes.

I like them when they are crisp and brown.

Finally, you can eat them. Last week we had them with tomato ketchup. They were great!

Illustrations © 2001, Sarah Warburton.

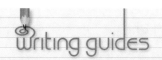

How to make a simple tent

● Cut out the diagrams and put them in the right order. Write instructions to go with each one.

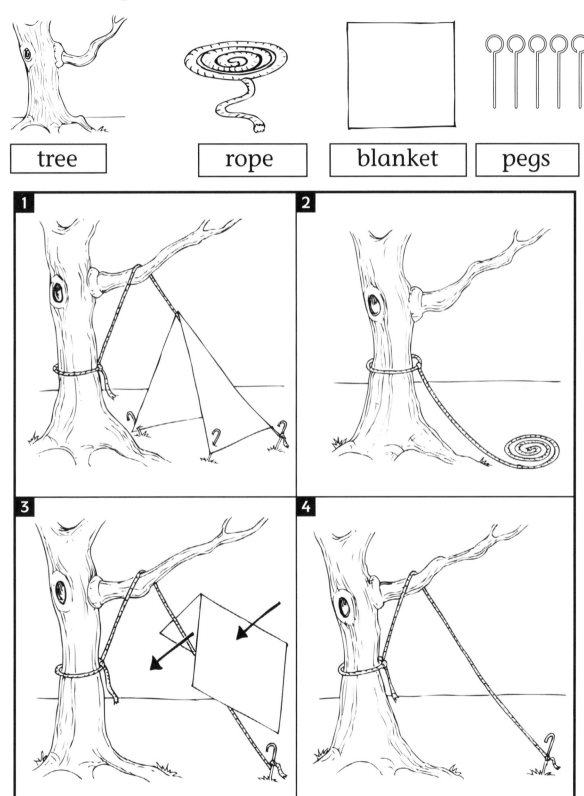

tree   rope   blanket   pegs

Illustrations © 2001, Sarah Warburton.

Section 2: Developing writing

Wiggling worms

● Read through these instructions carefully then answer the questions.

What to do

1. Find an old fish tank and make sure it is clean. This will become your wormery.

2. Fill the wormery with layers of different types of soil.

3. Water well.

4. Put in about 12 worms.

5. Put a thin layer of gravel on top and scatter dead leaves.

6. Cover the wormery with the cloth and leave for a few days.

7. Take a look. The worms will have mixed up the different layers of soil and pulled down the dried leaves.

8. Cover the wormery and look again every few days.

Learn all about how worms live!

Answer the following:

1. Will making a wormery be a clean or a messy job? _____

2. What problems might someone have in making a wormery?

_____

3. How long would it take to find out about how worms live?

_____

4. Write two sentences of information or advice to add to the instructions.

_____

_____

Illustrations © 2001, Sarah Warburton.

Now it's your turn...

● Read through the instructions carefully on photocopiable p32 then write a list of things you need.

How to make a wormery:

What you need

_____   _____

_____   _____

_____   _____

_____

● Match each of the following instructions with the correct diagram below.

Take a look. The worms will have mixed up the different layers of soil and pulled down the dried leaves.

Find an old fish tank and make sure it is clean. This will become your wormery.

Fill the wormery with layers of different types of soil.

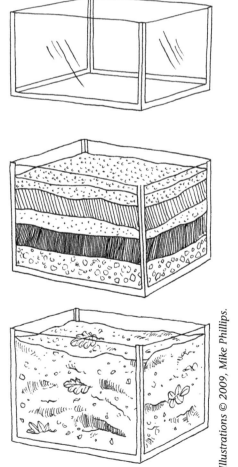

Illustrations © 2009, Mike Phillips.

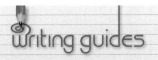

How to make mini pizzas

● Read this simple recipe, and use it as a reference for the CD-ROM activity.

Ingredients

1 plain muffin per persons
tomato sauce (not ketchup)
grated cheese
a selection of toppings, for example:
  • sweetcorn kernels
  • small pieces of ham
  • sliced tomato
  • sliced mushrooms and so on

Method

1. First toast the whole muffins for two minutes on each side.

2. Then cut them in half.

3. Spread some tomato sauce on the untoasted side of each half.

4. Scatter grated cheese over the tomato sauce.

5. Now, put on the toppings you like best.

6. Put pizzas under the grill for a few minutes until cheese has melted.

Illustrations © 2001, Sarah Warburton.

Section 3

Writing

This section helps the children to develop their writing by pulling together the work they have done so far. They will work on three extended activities that involve using the features they identified in Section 1 and drawing on the concepts they explored in Section 2.

Each activity will require several sessions in its planning, drafting and writing and you can use them in guided writing and for independent work. You can complete each activity using the photocopiables only or you can vary and extend them by using the templates and images provided on the CD-ROM.

When the children have drafted their instructions, they should give their first drafts to their writing partners to read through. They can do this in conjunction with photocopiable page 46 (peer evaluation sheet). Encourage the children to be critical in a constructive way. Ask them questions such as: *What is good about the instructions? What could be better or clearer? Has anything been missed out? Is the sequence of steps in the right order? Would any diagrams be helpful?*

The writers should then edit their instructions, taking their partners' comments into account. At this stage, encourage pupils to consider the layout and design of their instructions, helping them to see how these factors affect how easy or difficult the instructions are to follow. When they are happy with their text and layout, pupils can print out their text or make a neat copy to share with others.

Activities

The first activity presents a board-game template. The children will first plan the game – what happens and how to play it – and then draft instructions. As a class, you could go on to make a collection of games and offer them to other classes to play.

The second activity involves devising sets of instructions that relate to various aspects of school life. The aim is to produce a collection of instructions to help a new pupil. The children will consider the procedures involved in negotiating the school day or week, trying to see what is involved in each activity and communicating it in a set of simple instructions.

The book template can be used to make books in a variety of genres using ideas from other Scholastic writing guides.

The third activity invites the children to make their own little book by following a set of diagrams. They then write instructions to accompany the diagrams and finally make, write and illustrate their own book.

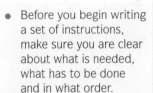

Writing tips

- Before you begin writing a set of instructions, make sure you are clear about what is needed, what has to be done and in what order.
- Write a title that explains what the instructions are about.
- List all of the equipment / materials needed.
- Use numbers, letters or bullet points to signal the order in which the steps need to be followed.
- Use short, concise sentences written in the imperative.
- Use diagrams, photographs and/or illustrations to support the instructions.
- Use adjectives and adverbs to clarify meaning rather than to describe.
- End the instructions with an appropriate closing statement.

Project 1: Crazy cat game

Objective

To develop and refine ideas in writing using planning and problem-solving strategies (Year 4, Strand 9).

What's on the CD-ROM

Crazy cat game
- Type notes and instructions about how to play the game.

Writing template
- Game template for writing detailed instructions under the headings 'What you need' and 'How to play'.

What to do

The aim of this activity is for the children to work in pairs to decide how a game is played and then write two types of instructions – those that tell you how to play the game before you start and those that tell you what to do as you go around the board.

If children are unfamiliar with the conventions of this type of board game, you can make opportunities for them to play one or two, such as Snakes and Ladders. In a shared session, explore some of the typical features, such as rolling dice and counting along squares.

Discuss different types of playing instructions – those that tell you how to play the game before you start and those that tell you what to do as you go around the board (for example, miss a turn, move on two spaces and so on).

- Hand out sheets of photocopiable pages 38 and 39, printed out onto A3. As a class, talk about how a game might be played.

- Explain that the boxes with thicker outlines feature illustrations that tell you what to do. Organise the children into pairs and start by coming up with ideas about mischievous and well-behaved things that the crazy cat might do, and incidents that happen. The bad things will probably be funnier and more interesting than the good (for example 'gets stuck in a washing machine' or 'chases the dog next door'), but encourage the children to put in a few good things to help the game to progress.

- Remind them that players are usually held up when they land on a 'bad' square and moved on (or given an extra go) when they land on something 'good'.

- Look at the instruction on square 3. Open the CD-ROM file 'Crazy Cat Game' and ask the children to type in instructions for each illustration; or they can write their instructions on the photocopiable sheet. They can also draw their own illustrations in the outlined boxes on the sheet.

- Look at the last screen of the CD-ROM file. This invites the children to write about how to play the game. Together, read the prompts on the screen and then ask the children to type in ideas of how the game should be played.
  They should consider points such as:
  – What things make you move on?
  – How do you score?
  – What happens when you land on a square with an instruction?
  – Where do you finish?

- Using the game template on the CD-ROM ask the children to write their own detailed instructions on how to play the game.

- Display a photo-enlarged copy of the evaluation questions on page 46, 'Peer review' to help them in their final task. Ask the children to edit their work, then give their instructions to another pair and ask them to test them out.

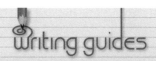

Project 2: Guide for a new pupil

What to do

This activity requires the children to write instructions to help a new child joining their class.

- Remind the children of some of the things they do every day in class and help them to see how complicated it might seem to someone new.

- Explain that you would like them to write instructions for a range of things that they do during the school week.

- Put the children inot pairs or groups. Open the CD-ROM file 'Guide for a new pupil' and ask the children to type in answers to the questions to help them plan their guide. Alternatively photocopy pages 40 and 41 onto A3 paper and let the children fill in the sheets by hand. Replace any topics that don't apply with alternatives.

- Next, go to the 'My instructions' button and open the guide book writing template. Explain that the aim is to print out a completed guide or booklet for a new child at school. Invite the children to use their notes to fill out each section. They can add more template pages if needed and can also upload and add their own images into the template.

Project 3: How to make a book

What to do

The children write instructions for making a book. They can make their book by hand or print it out from the CD-ROM.

- Give a copy of photocopiable page 42 to pairs of children. Tell them that the written instructions are missing and ask them to work out how to make a book using the diagrams only. They will need a piece of A3 paper, stapler and scissors.

- Ask: *Would the task have been easier with written instructions?*

- Open the CD-ROM file 'How to make a book' and ask the children to add written instructions to accompany the diagrams on the screen. Alternatively, they can cut out the diagrams from the photocopiable sheet, glue them to another piece of paper and write the instructions underneath each one.

- Another pair should evaluate and edit their instructions.

- Next, go the 'Planning' button on the CD-ROM or hand out copies of photocopiable p43 and let the children plan the instrcutions for their chosen topic, for example 'How to look after a puppy'.

- The children should then make their own book using the diagrams on the photocpiable sheet and write their topic instructions into it by hand. Alternatively they can complete the mini book writing template (found in the 'My instructions' section) and type in their instructions.

Photocopiable SCHOLASTIC
www.scholastic.co.uk

Crazy cat game

9	8	7 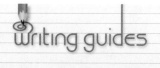	6	5

10 _____

_____

_____

10
11
12

7 _____

_____

_____

_____

13

13 _____

_____

_____

14 _____

_____

_____

14

15	16	17	18	1

18 _____

_____

_____

3 _Sleep by the fire. Move on two spaces_

4	3	2	1

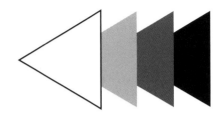

30	29	28	27

27 _____

_____

_____

_____

_____

26

25

24 _____

_____

_____

24

20	21	22	23

21 _____

_____

_____

Guide for a new pupil

- What does a new pupil need to know when they start in your class?
- Use the following questions to help you to make notes.

What time should you arrive in the morning?

_____

What things make your teacher happy?

_____

_____

_____

What things make your teacher cross?

_____

_____

_____

What do you do at playtime?

_____

_____

_____

_____

_____

What do you do with:

- your coat? _____

_____

_____

- your bag? _____

_____

_____

- your lunch? _____

_____

_____

Illustrations © 2009, Mike Phillips.

What do you do at lunchtime?

_____

_____

_____

_____

_____

What happens when it rains at playtime?

_____

_____

_____

What do you do when you have:

- swimming? _____

_____

_____

- library? _____

_____

_____

- PE? _____

_____

_____

- cooking? _____

_____

_____

Are there any rules for parents?

_____

Where do adults wait at home time?

_____

Where should they park their cars?

_____

Are there any other rules?

_____

_____

_____

How to make a book

● With a partner, follow these diagrams to make a book. Then, write a set of instructions to accompany the diagrams.

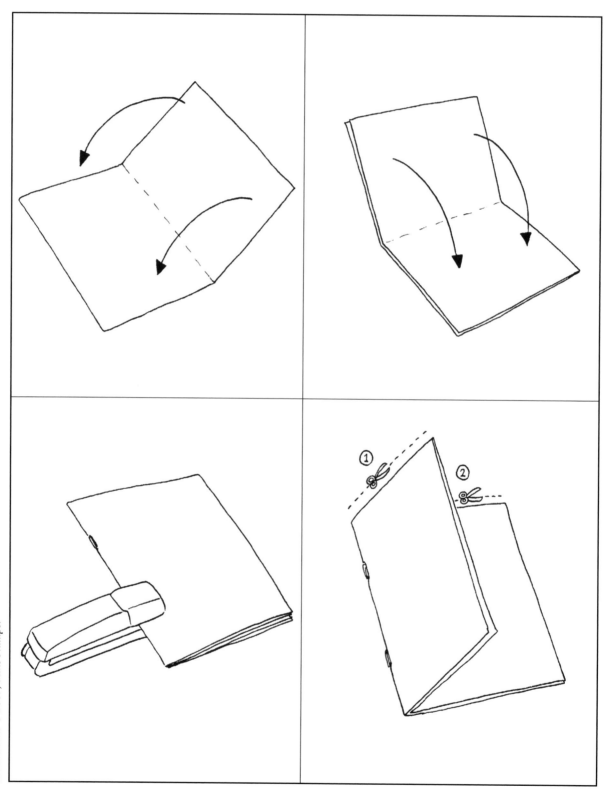

Planning tips for an instruction book

● Now you have made your own instrcution book, decide what the topic will be about, for example 'How to look after a puppy'.

● Use the following questions to help you to make notes about your topic before you start writing down your instructions.

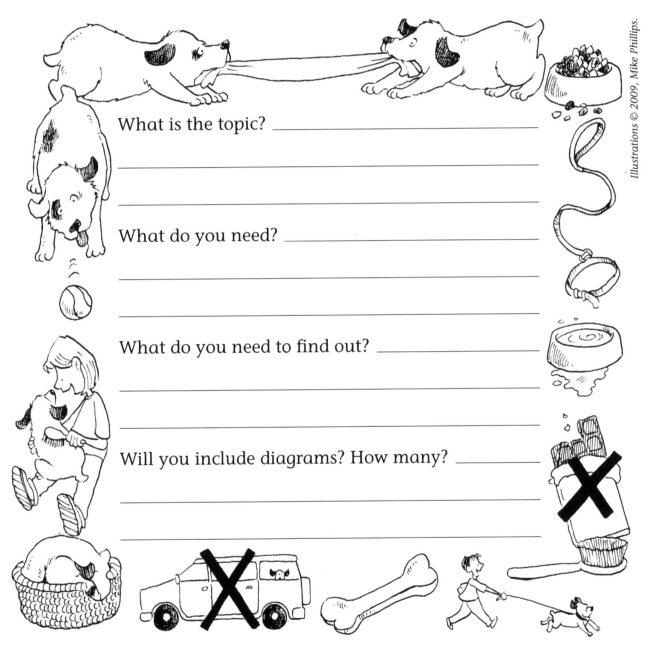

What is the topic? _____

_____

_____

What do you need? _____

_____

_____

What do you need to find out? _____

_____

_____

Will you include diagrams? How many? _____

_____

_____

Illustrations © 2009, Mike Phillips.

● You have four pages for the instructions in your book. Decide what you will put on each page. You will need a title, and then some or all of the following: a step-by-step guide, a list of what you need, tips and information.

Section 4

Review

This section helps the children to identify the strengths and weaknesses of the instructions work that has been produced – their own and that of others. It also provides you with opportunities to review how well the children have understood what is required when writing instructions and also to evaluate their progress against a variety of objectives.

Self- and peer review

'Self-review' (photocopiable page 45) helps the children to evaluate their own work in progress. Explain that revision is not necessarily something that you save for the end of a piece of work. Experienced writers look critically at their work while it is in progress and make revisions as they go along. It is often easier to do this when the work is in draft form.

Point out that this sheet highlights some of the criteria for evaluating their own work. Explain that if they pause during their writing and ask themselves these questions they will see how they are doing and be able to edit and improve their work.

The children can use 'Peer review' (photocopiable page 46) as an exercise to review a first draft or a final version of their partner's work or of their own writing. Encourage the children to work with partners throughout the writing process, sharing their first drafts and talking through each section of their writing. The questions on the sheet are intended to help the children to appreciate the significant aspects of instruction writing and to be constructively critical in their responses.

Teacher review

You can use the objectives on photocopiable page 47 as a checklist to assess the work of individual children and as a list of goals which illustrate the way forward. Individual objectives can provide the basis for a discussion with each child in which you look at examples of work, highlighting progress and agreeing on the way forward. Advice should point to the most immediate action to be taken to bring about improvement.

It is important to provide the children with feedback on their most recent piece of work which will bridge the gap between their current performance and the desired goal. Try to ensure your feedback is positive and encouraging while highlighting a specific action for improvement.

When forming an overall assessment of the child's progress, you may wish to check work in progress against the criteria as well as looking at finished texts; also look back at work from Sections 1 and 2 to check their understanding of individual aspects of instructional writing and to find evidence of their achievements in tasks where outcomes were limited.

In relation to reviewing the activities worked through in Section 3, you may wish to take into account the children's initial drafts and how successfully they worked in pairs or groups. It is also important to assess the work in terms of the generic features of instructions that were identified in Section 1 and explored in more detail in Section 2.

Self review

● Look at your draft instructions. Ask yourself these questions and put a tick or a cross in each box. Use your responses to help you to revise your work.

My instructions tell the reader:

what the aim is ☐

what they will need ☐

what to do ☐

I have used:

imperative verbs ☐ for example _____

time connectives ☐ for example _____

short sentences ☐

diagrams ☐

I think my layout:

is clear ☐

It might be clearer if I _____

I think my series of steps are:

in a sensible order ☐

expressed simply and clearly ☐

My instructions would be better if I _____

_____

_____

Illustrations © 2001, Sarah Warburton.

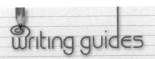

Peer review

1. Does the title tell you clearly what the instructions are for? _____

2. Is it clear what you will need? _____

3. Is everything used? _____

4. Are the instructions written as a list for you to follow? _____

5. Is the series of steps in a sensible order? _____

    - If *no*, how would you change them? _____

6. Are there any imperative verbs? _____

    - If *yes*, give two examples. _____

    - If *no*, give two examples of verbs used: _____

    - What tense are the verbs in? _____

7. Are any sentences too long? _____

    - If *yes*, give an example: _____

    _____

8. Are any sentences unclear? _____

    - If so, give an example: _____

    _____

9. Would you change or add any diagrams? Say why: _____

    _____

10. What else do you think could be done better? _____

    _____

Teacher review

	AF5 Vary sentences for clarity, purpose and effect	AF6 Write with technical accuracy of syntax and punctuation in phrases, clauses and sentences.	AF3 Organise and present whole texts effectively, sequencing and structuring information, ideas and events	AF4 Construct paragraphs and use cohesion within and between paragraphs	AF1 Write imaginative interesting and thoughtful texts	AF2 Produce texts that are appropriate to the task, reader and purpose	AF7 Select appropriate and effective vocabulary
LEVEL 2	Mostly simple sentences with clauses joined by and. A variety of time connectives and or imperative verbs used to vary sentence openings. Present tense generally used consistently.	Use of full stops and capital letters to demarcate sentences is generally accurate. Clauses are grammatically accurate. Some accurate use of commas to separate items in a list.	Attempts to use an appropriate system to organise ideas, e.g. bullet points, a numbered list. Some time related words and phrases are used to sequence ideas.	Instructions written as a series of points set out in a list. May be some linking of ideas using time connectives, e.g. next, then.	Content generally relevant to the instructions being given. Some apt word choices create interest.	Some features of instructional texts are used appropriately in own writing, e.g. numbered list, short simple sentences. Attempts to use appropriate writing style.	Use of appropriate vocabulary including some imperative verbs 'mix' 'stir'.
LEVEL 3	Imperative verbs used consistently throughout piece of writing. Some variation in sentence structure but overall succinct sentences. Consistent use of present tense throughout writing.	Use of full stops, capital letters, exclamation marks and question marks to demarcate sentences is accurate. Commas are used accurately in lists. Some use of commas to mark clauses.	Instructions are written in chronological order. Opening and closings sometimes signalled appropriately. (Your kite is now ready to fly. Have fun!) Subheadings may be used to support layout(E.g. Method, Equipment)	Instructions are broken down into clear sections 'You will need' 'What to do' Text is presented clearly using e.g. bullet points, numbers, letters to signal the order in which steps need to be followed.	Content and ideas are appropriate to the task. Some additional advice or comments may be given 'If the mixture is too runny...'	Attempts to write in an appropriate style, demonstrating some awareness of reader, e.g. 'your seeds' 'choose the spread you prefer' Instructions are clear and succinct.	Imperative verbs used throughout the text. Vocabulary is appropriate to task with some variation. Some adjectives and adverbs used to clarify meaning 'carefully' 'slowly'